A PICTORIAL STORY OF JAMESTOWN, VIRGINIA:

THE VOYAGE AND SEARCH FOR A SETTLEMENT SITE

By

J. PAUL HUDSON

Arms of the
Virginia Company of London

Illustrated by Sidney E. King

Events Which Occurred From the
Time the Colonists Left England, December 20, 1606,
Until
They Landed at Jamestown, May 13-14, 1607.
Based on Contemporary Sources

LIBRARY OF CONGRESS CATALOG NUMBER: 57-11468

PRINTED IN THE U. S. A. BY GARRETT and MASSIE, INC., Richmond, Virginia.

King James I of England, after whom Jamestown, Virginia was named. On April 10, 1606, King James granted a charter to the Virginia Company of London —making possible the establishment of the first successful English colony in the New World. Portrait by Daniel Mytens, 1621. Reproduced through courtesy of National Portrait Gallery, London.

To Ethel,
My Sweet and Understanding Wife

DEDICATION

This book is dedicated to the 105 brave Englishmen who planted the first successful English colony in the New World, especially 67 of this group who died during the first autumn and winter. The names of the adventurers who braved the wilderness and established the colony are:

HENRY ADLING, Gentleman
JEREMY ALICOCK, Gentleman
GABRIEL ARCHER, Captain, Gentleman
JOHN ASBIE
BENJAMIN BEAST, Gentleman
ROBERT BEHETHLAND, Gentleman
EDWARD BRINTO, Mason, Soldier
EDWARD BROOKES, Gentleman. Died of heat exhaustion and thirst, Island of Mona, West Indies, April 7, 1607.
JOHN BROOKES, Gentleman
EDWARD BROWNE, Gentleman
JAMES BRUMFIELD, Boy
WILLIAM BRUSTER, Gentleman
JOHN CAPPER
GEORGE CASSEN, Labourer
THOMAS CASSEN, Labourer
WILLIAM CASSEN, Labourer
EUSTACE CLOVILL, Gentleman
SAMUELL COLLIER, Boy
ROGER COOKE, Gentleman
THOMAS COWPER, Barber
RICHARD CROFTS, Gentleman
RICHARD DIXON, Gentleman
JOHN DODS, Labourer, Soldier
OLD EDWARD, Labourer
THOMAS EMRY, Carpenter
ROBERT FENTON, Gentleman
GEORGE FLOWER, Gentleman
ROBERT FORD, Gentleman
RICHARD FRITH, Gentleman
STEPHEN GALTHORPE
WILLIAM GARRET, Bricklayer
GEORGE GOULDING, Labourer
THOMAS GORE, Gentleman
ANTHONY GOSNOLD, Gentleman
ANTHONY GOSNOLL, Gentleman
BARTHOLOMEW GOSNOLD, Captain, Councilor
THOMAS GOWER, Gentleman
STEPHEN HALTHROP, Gentleman
EDWARD HARRINGTON, Gentleman
JOHN HERD, Bricklayer
NICHOLAS HOULGRAVE, Gentleman
ROBERT HUNT, Master, Preacher, Gentleman
THOMAS JACOB, Sergeant
WILLIAM JOHNSON, Labourer
GEORGE KENDALL, Captain, Councilor

ELLIS KINGSTON, Gentleman
WILLIAM LAXON, Carpenter
JOHN LAYDON, Labourer
WILLIAM LOVE, Tailor
JOHN MARTIN, Captain, Councilor
JOHN MARTIN, Gentleman
GEORGE MARTIN, Gentleman
FRANCIS MIDWINTER, Gentleman
EDWARD MORISH, Gentleman, Corporal
THOMAS MOUNSLIC
THOMAS MOUTON
RICHARD MUTTON, Boy
NATHANIEL PECOCK, Boy, Soldier
JOHN PENINGTON, Gentleman
GEORGE PERCY, Master, Gentleman
DRU PICKHOUSE, Gentleman
EDWARD PISING, Carpenter
NATHANIELL POWELL, Gentleman
JONAS PROFIT, Sailor
JOHN RATCLIFFE, Captain, Councilor
JAMES READ, Blacksmith
JEHU ROBINSON, Gentleman
WILLIAM RODS, Labourer
THOMAS SANDS, Gentleman
JOHN SHORT, Gentleman
RICHARD SIMONS, Gentleman
NICHOLAS SKOT, Drummer
ROBERT SMALL, Carpenter
WILLIAM SMETHES, Gentleman
JOHN SMITH, Captain, Councilor
FRANCIS SNARSBROUGH, Gentleman
JOHN STEVENSON, Gentleman
THOMAS STUDLEY, Gentleman
WILLIAM TANKARD, Gentleman
HENRY TAVIN, Labourer
KELLAM THROGMORTON, Gentleman
ANAS TODKILL, Soldier
WILLIAM UNGER, Labourer
JOHN WALLER, Gentleman
GEORGE WALKER, Gentleman
THOMAS WEBBE, Gentleman
WILLIAM WHITE, Labourer
WILLIAM WILKINSON, Surgeon
EDWARD MARIA WINGFIELD, Master, Councilor, President
THOMAS WOTTON, Gentleman, Surgeon
"with diverse others, to the number of 105."

INTRODUCTION

ESTABLISHMENT OF THE VIRGINIA COMPANY OF LONDON

On April 10, 1606, King James I granted a charter to the Virginia Company of London. The charter designated the territory available for settlement as that lying between the 34th and 45th degrees of north latitude, "and the islands thereunto adjacent, or within one hundred miles of the coasts thereof." The Virginia Company raised funds (by issuing stock) for the New World expedition, which would never have been possible without such backing.

REASONS FOR FOUNDING A COLONY IN THE NEW WORLD

There were many reasons why the Virginia Company wished to establish a colony in America. The members of the Company, who were stockholders, naturally expected a good return on their investments. Secondly, they wished to establish a settlement in Virginia where English goods could be shipped in exchange for New World commodities. Thirdly, and specified in the charter from the king, the colonists were to propagate the "Christian religion to such people [the Indians], as yet live in darkness and miserable ignorance of the true knowledge and worship of God. . . ." The charter also encouraged them to search for mineral wealth—"to dig, mine, and search for all manner of mines of gold, silver, and copper. . . ."

Other reasons for establishing the colony:

To find a route to the "East India [South] Sea."

To search for Sir Walter Raleigh's ill-fated colony of 1587.

To establish a foothold in North America, which, in turn, would bar the further spread of Spain and France between the 34th and 45th degrees of north latitude.

To find as many commodities and crops as possible which the English were forced to purchase from European nations at exorbitant prices. The Colonists were asked specifically to search for furs, cordage, masts, planks, boards, pitch, tar, potash, soap ashes, hemp, flax, iron, grapes and other fruits, salt, silk, roots and berries, medicinal plants and herbs, sweet woods, oils and gums, cotton, silk-grass, sugar cane, and grains.

The settlers of the yeoman class who did not own stock in the Virginia Company were drawn overseas in order to better themselves, which, in the seventeenth century, meant to acquire a small tract of land.

LONDON IN 1606

In 1606, when the Virginia colonists left London, the city had a population of approximately 250,000. By its size, wealth and power it was the largest and most formidable city in the kingdom.

The Voyage

"... one of the most important voyages in world history."—Matthew Page Andrews.

THE COLONISTS LEAVE LONDON

December 19-20, 1606.

On a bleak December day, a week before Christmas, 105 colonists and 39 mariners sailed from Blackwall in three small ships—the *Susan Constant* of 100 tons (commanded by Captain Christopher Newport, carrying 71 persons); the *Godspeed* of 40 tons (commanded by Captain Bartholomew Gosnold, carrying 52 persons); and the *Discovery* (a pinnace of 20 tons commanded by Captain John Ratcliffe, carrying 21 persons).

Unfavorable winds, however, kept the small fleet in sight of England for approximately six weeks, as reported by several members of the expedition:

"On the 19 of December, 1606. we set saile, but by unprosperous winds, were kept six weekes in the sight of England; all which time, Maister Hunt our Preacher, was so weake and sicke, that few expected his recoverie."[1]

Master George Percy (member of the first colony, councilor, brother of the Earl of Northumberland) gave the date of departure as December 20:

"On Saturday the twentieth of December in the yeere of 1606. the fleet fell from London, and the fift of Ianuary we anchored in the Downes; but the winds continued contrarie so long, that we were forced to stay there some time, where wee suffered great stormes, but by the skilfulnesse of the Captaine we suffered no great losse or danger."[2]

[1]*The Proceedings of the English Colonie in Virginia since their first beginning from England in the yeare of our Lord 1606, till this present 1612, with all their accidents that befell them in their Iournies and Discoveries,* by Thomas Studley, Anas Todkill, Nathaniell Powell, and others (Oxford, 1612).

[2]*Observations gathered out of a Discourse of the Plantation of the Southerne Colonie in Virginia by the English, 1606: Written by that Honorable Gentleman, Master George Percy.* From the Rev. Samuel Purchas, *Pilgrimes,* iv, 1685-1690, edition 1625.

[1]

A STORM

February 12, 1607.

As the small fleet remained within sight of England for six weeks it was near the end of January (or early February) before favorable winds blew and sent the three ships on their way. George Percy reported:

"The twelfth day of February at night we saw a blazing Starre, and presently a storme."

ARRIVAL AT THE CANARY ISLANDS

Late February or early March, 1607.

The colonists' first stop was at the Canary Islands, off the northwest coast of Africa, where they took on fresh water. Percy did not mention this visit, and John Smith commented on it only briefly:

"You shall understand that after many crosses in the downes by tempests, wee arrived safely uppon the Southwest part of the great Canaries . . ."[3]

The writers of *The Proceedings of the English Colonie in Virginia . . .* described the stop at the Canaries in few words:

"Wee watred at the Canaries . . ."

[3] *A True Relation of such occurrences and accidents of noate as hath hapned in Virginia since the first planting of that Collony, which is now resident in the South part thereof, till the last returne from thence. Written by Captaine Smith, Coronell of the said Collony, to a worshipfull friend of his in England* (London, 1608).

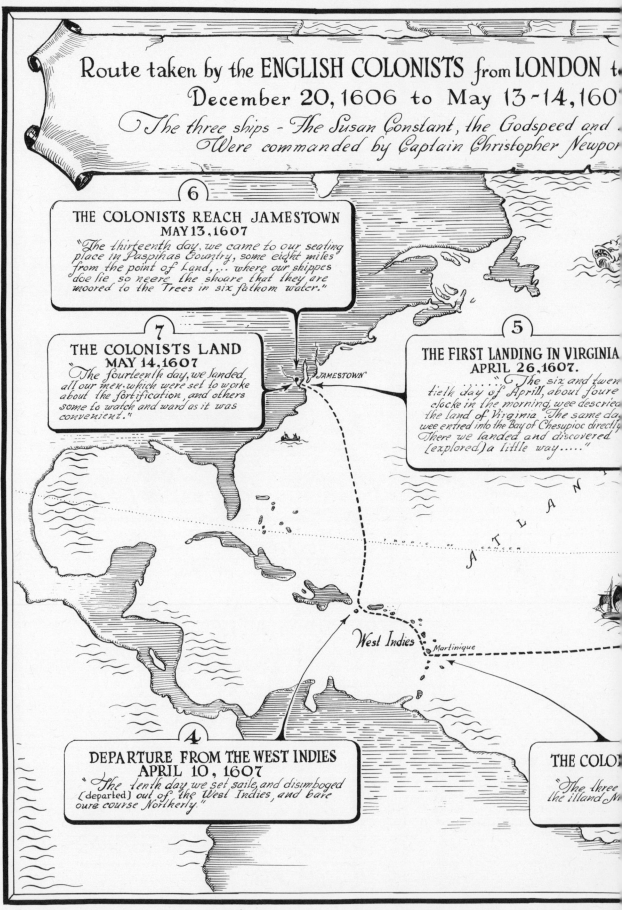

Route taken by the ENGLISH COLONISTS from LONDON t•
December 20, 1606 to May 13~14, 160⁊
The three ships - The Susan Constant, the Godspeed and
Were commanded by Captain Christopher Newpor⁊

6

THE COLONISTS REACH JAMESTOWN
MAY 13, 1607

"The thirteenth day, we came to our seating place in Paspihas Country, some eight miles from the point of Land, ... where our shippes doe lie so neere the shoare that they are moored to the Trees in six fathom water."

7

THE COLONISTS LAND
MAY 14, 1607

"The fourteenth day, we landed all our men which were set to worke about the fortification, and others some to watch and ward as it was convenient."

5

THE FIRST LANDING IN VIRGINIA
APRIL 26, 1607.

"The six and twentieth day of Aprill, about foure clocke in the morning, wee descried the land of Virginia. The same day wee entred into the Bay of Chesupioc directly. There we landed and discovered (explored) a little way....."

JAMESTOWN

West Indies   Martinique

4

DEPARTURE FROM THE WEST INDIES
APRIL 10, 1607

"The tenth day we set saile, and disimboged (departed) out of the West Indies, and bare oure course Northerly."

THE COLO⁊

"The three
the illand M

TROPIC OF CANCER   ATLANTI

The quotations are from George Percy's "Observations gathered out of a Discourse of the Plantatio
Percy was a member of the first Colony, and remaine⁊

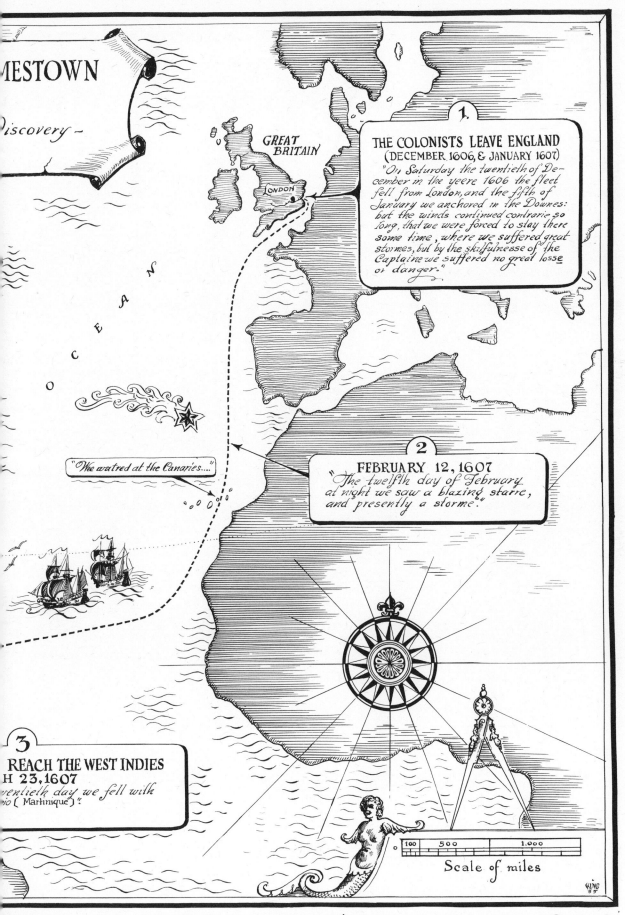

MESTOWN

Discovery –

GREAT
BRITAIN

LONDON

1.
THE COLONISTS LEAVE ENGLAND
(DECEMBER 1606, & JANUARY 1607)
"On Saturday the twentieth of December in the yeere 1606 the fleet fell from London, and the fifth of January we anchored in the Downes: but the winds continued contrarie so long, that we were forced to stay there some time, where we suffered great stormes, but by the skilfulnesse of the Captaine we suffered no great losse or danger."

OCEAN

"Wee watred at the Canaries...."

2
FEBRUARY 12, 1607
"The twelfth day of February at night we saw a blazing starre, and presently a storme."

3
REACH THE WEST INDIES
H 23, 1607
ventieth day we fell with
io (Martinique)".

100   500   1,000
Scale of miles

KING
35

the Southerne Colonie in Virginia by the English, 1606," published in 1625 by Samuel Purchas.
Jamestown until April 22, 1612.

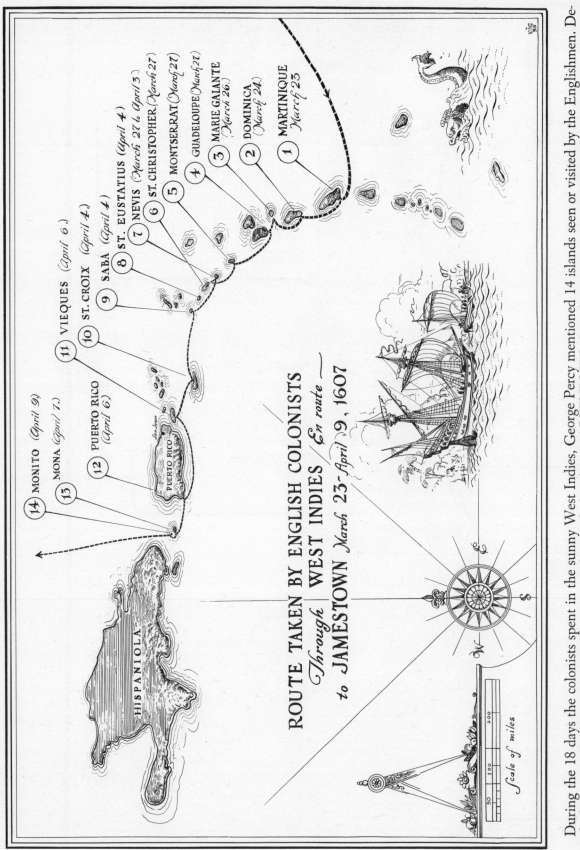

ROUTE TAKEN BY ENGLISH COLONISTS
Through WEST INDIES *En route*
to JAMESTOWN *March 23-April 9*, 1607

(1) MARTINIQUE *March 23*
(2) DOMINICA *(March 24.)*
(3) MARIE GALANTE *(March 26.)*
(4) GUADELOUPE *(March 27.)*
(5) MONTSERRAT *(March 27.)*
(6) ST. CHRISTOPHER *(March 27.)*
(7) NEVIS *(March 27 to April 3.)*
(8) ST. EUSTATIUS *(April 4.)*
(9) SABA *(April 4.)*
(10) ST. CROIX *(April 4.)*
(11) VIEQUES *(April 6.)*
(12) PUERTO RICO *(April 6.)*
(13) MONA *(April 7.)*
(14) MONITO *(April 9.)*

HISPANIOLA

PUERTO RICO

Scale of miles
50   100   200

During the 18 days the colonists spent in the sunny West Indies, George Percy mentioned 14 islands seen or visited by the Englishmen. Described in some detail on the following pages, they include: (1) MARTINIQUE–March 23. (2) DOMINICA–March 24. (3) MARIE GALANTE–March 26. (4) GUADELOUPE–March 27. (5) MONTSERRAT–March 27. (6) ST. CHRISTOPHER–March 27. (7) NEVIS–March 27 to April 3. (8) ST. EUSTATIUS–April 4. (9) SABA–April 4. (10) VIRGIN ISLANDS (ST. CROIX)–April 4. (11) VIEQUES–April 6. (12) PUERTO RICO–April 6. (13) MONA–April 7. (14) MONITO–April 9.

ARRIVAL IN THE WEST INDIES (MARTINIQUE-1)

March 23, 1607.

Three months after boarding the ships in England the colonists arrived in the West Indies. The first island sighted was Martinique:

"The three and twentieth day [of March] we fell with the Iland of Mattanenio *[Martinique] in the West Indies."*

—George Percy, *Observations*

John Smith and Thomas Studley, in their writings, do not mention the sighting of Martinique.

It appears that the small fleet of three ships did not stop at Martinique Island but continued on to the Island of Dominica, where a landing was made the following day.

[7]

Trading With the Indians

A STOP AT DOMINICA (2): FIRST ENCOUNTER WITH THE INDIANS

March 24, 1607.

This was an eventful day for the colonists—their first landing since leaving the Canaries and their first glimpse of the "Savage Indians." Still 1400 miles from the American mainland, the Virginia-bound settlers at Dominica must have sensed for the first time that they were in a strange and new world. George Percy related the day's event with clarity, especially his description of the stone-age aborigines:

"The foure and twentieth day we anchored at Dominico, within fourteene degrees of the Line, a very faire Iland, the Trees full of sweet and good smels inhabited by many Savage Indians, they were at first very scrupulous to come aboord us. Wee learned of them afterwards that the Spaniards had given them a great overthrow on this Ile, but when they knew what we were, there came many to our ships with their Canoas, bringing us many kindes of sundry fruites, as Pines [pineapples], Potatoes, Plantons [bananas], Tobacco, and other fruits, and Roane Cloth [leather] abundance, which they had gotten out of certaine Spanish ships that were cast away upon that Iland. We gave them

Knives, Hatchets for exchange which they esteeme much, wee also gave them Beades, Copper Jewels which they hang through their nosthrils, ears, and lips, very strange to behold.

"Their bodies are all painted red, to keepe away the biting of Muscetos. They goe all naked without covering. The haire of their head is a yard long, all of a length, pleated in three plats hanging downe to their wastes. They suffer no haire to grow on their faces. They cut [tattoo] their skinnes in divers workes [patterns]. They are continually in warres; and will eate their enemies when they kill them, or any stranger if they take them. They will lap up mans spittle, whilst one spits in their mouthes, in a barbarous fashion like Dogges . . . These people doe poyson their Arrow heads, which are made of a fishes bone. They worship the Devill for their God, and have no other beliefe. . . ."

Thomas Studley and his collaborators briefly mentioned the stop at Dominico: ". . . wee traded with the Salvages at Dominica. . . ."

Boiling pork in a hot
spring at Guadeloupe.

GUADELOUPE ISLAND (4)

March 27, 1607.

On this day the colonists reached the island of
Guadeloupe, where they went ashore for a short time
and found a hot spring:

"... *the next day [27 March], wee sailed with a
slacke saile, alongst the Ile of Guadalupa; where we
went ashore, and found a Bath [spring] which was so
hot that no man was able to stand long by it. Our Ad-
mirall, Captaine* Newport, *caused a piece of Porke to
be put in it; which boyled it so, in the space of halfe
an hour, as no fire could mend it. ...*"

—George Percy, *Observations*

ISLAND OF MARIE GALANTE (3)

March 26, 1607.

From Dominica the fleet sailed northward, passing
by the island of Marie Galante on March 26:

"*The sixe and twentieth day, we had sight of Mari-
galanta. ...*"

—George Percy, *Observations*

Bathing at Nevis.

MONTSERRAT (5),
ST. CHRISTOPHER (6),
AND NEVIS (7)

March 27-28, 1607.

From Guadeloupe the ships sailed in a northwesterly direction, passing by the islands of Montserrat and St. Christopher, and on to the island of Nevis. At Nevis all the men landed, where they encamped for six days. Accustomed to the damp climate and fogs of England, the warmth and exotic scenery of the colorful island must have pleased the subjects of King James. Percy described their experiences:

"Then we went aboord [at Guadeloupe], and sailed by many Ilands, as Mounserot and an Iland called Saint Christopher; both uninhabited.

"About two a clocke in the afternoone [28 March], wee anchored at the Ile of Mevis [Nevis]. There the Captaine landed all his men, being well fitted with Muskets and other convenient Armes; marched a mile into the Woods: being commanded to stand upon their guard, fearing the treacherie of the Indians; which is an ordinary use amongst them, and all other Savages on this Ile. We came to a Bath [spring] standing in a Valley betwixt two Hils, where wee bathed our selves; and found it to be of the nature of the Bathes in England, some places hot and some colder: and men may refresh themselves as they please.

"Finding this place to be so convenient for our men to avoid diseases which will breed in so long a Voyage, wee incamped ourselves on this Ile six dayes, and spent none of our ships victuall, by reason our men, some went a hunting, some a fouling, and some a fishing: where we got great store of Conies [rabbits or hares], sundry kinds of fowles, and great plentie of fish. We kept Centinels and Courts de gard at every Captaines quarter, fearing wee should be assaulted by the Indians, that were on the other side of the Iland. We saw none, nor were molested by any: but some few we saw as we were a hunting on the Iland. They would not come to us by any meanes, but ranne swiftly through the Woods to the Mountaine tops, so we lost the sight of them: whereupon we made all the haste wee could to our quarter, thinking there had beene a great ambush of Indians there abouts.

"We past into the thickest of the Woods, where we had almost lost our selves. We had not gone above halfe a mile amongst the thicke, but we came into a most pleasant Garden: being a hundred paces square on every side, having many Cotton-trees growing in it with abundance of Cotton-wooll, and many Guiacum trees. Wee saw the goodliest tall trees growing so thicke about the Garden, as though they had been set by Art: which made us marvell very much to see it."

April 3, 1607.—Departure from Nevis (7)

"The third day, we set saile from Mevis."

—George Percy, Observations

[10]

Catching fish and sea tortoises at the Virgin Islands.

ST. EUSTATIUS (8), SABA (9), AND THE "ILE OF VIRGINES (10)"

April 4, 1607.

After leaving the island of Nevis the fleet passed by St. Eustatius and Saba, and then anchored at one of the Virgin Islands—probably St. Croix. Fishing was good, many sea tortoises were caught, and fowls were killed in great numbers. Some of the men tasted a bark resembling cinnamon but, as Percy related, there was no fresh water on the island to quench their thirst:

"This day, we anchored at the Ile of Virgines, in an excellent Bay able to harbour a hundred Ships. If this Bay stood in England, it would be a great profit and commoditie to the Land. On this Iland wee caught great store of Fresh-fish and abundance of Sea Tortoises, which served all our Fleet three daies, which
were in number eight score persons. Wee also killed great store of wilde Fowle. Wee cut the Barkes of certaine Trees which tasted much like Cinnamon, and very hot in the mouth. This Iland in some places hath very good ground, straight and tall Timber. But the greatest discommoditie that wee have seen on this Iland is that it hath no Fresh-water, which makes the place void of any Inhabitants."

Easter Sunday—April 5—was spent in the Virgin Islands, probably at or near St. Croix.

April 6, 1607.—The colonists sail by Vieques (11) and Puerto Rico (12)

[11]

ARRIVAL AT MONA (13), LOSS OF EDWARD BROOKES, GENTLEMAN

April 7, 1607.

The warm spring days in the West Indies must have been pleasant ones for the colonists as they sailed westward past Vieques and along the south shore of the island of Puerto Rico. All seemed to go well until the ships anchored at Mona. While exploring the interior of this small island during a hot and oppressive day, the first Englishman, Edward Brookes, Gentleman, died. Percy related the adventures of the brave men:

April 7, 1607

"Many of our men fainted in the march,"...

Death of Edward Brooks at Mona.

"Upon the sixt day, we set saile and passed by Becam [Vieques], and by Saint John de Porto Rico. The seventh day, we arrived at Mona: where wee watered, which wee stood in great need of, seeing that our water did smell so vildly that none of our men was able to indure it. Whilst some of the Saylers were a filling the Caskes with water, the Captaine, and the rest of the Gentlemen, and other Soldiers marched up in the Ile sixe myles, thinking to find some other provision to maintaine our victualling; as wee marched we killed two wild Bores, and saw a huge wild Bull, his hornes was an ell [45 inches] betweene the two tops. Wee also killed Guanas, in fashion of a Serpent, and speckled like a Toade under the belly. These wayes that wee went, being so troublesome and vilde going upon the sharpe Rockes, that many of our men fainted in the march, but by good fortune wee lost none but one Edward Brookes Gentleman, whose fat melted within him by the great heate and drought of the Countrey: we were not able to relieve him nor our selves, so he died in that great extreamitie."

Thomas Studley and his collaborators did not mention the death of Brookes. They did, however, comment on the iguana, birds, and fish:

"In Mevis, Mona, and the Virgin Iles, we spent some time, where with a lothsome beast like a Crocadil, called a Gwayn [Iguana], Tortoses, Pellicans, Parrots, and fishes, we daily feasted."

[12]

THE ISLE OF, MONITO (14), LAST STOP IN THE WEST INDIES

April 9, 1607.

The last place the colonists visited in the West Indies was the small Isle of Monito, located between Puerto Rico and present-day Dominican Republic. The abundance of bird life on the small island attracted the attention of the settlers as narrated by both George Percy and Thomas Studley:

Gathering eggs at Monito.

"The ninth day in the afternoone, we went off with our Boat to the Ile of Moneta, some three leagues from Mona, where we had a terrible landing, and a troublesome getting up to the top of the Mountaine or Ile, being a high firme Rocke step, with many terrible sharpe stones: After wee got to the top of the Ile, we found it to bee a fertill and plaine ground, full of goodly grasse, and abundance of Fowles of all kindes, they flew over our heads as thicke as drops of Hale; besides they made such a noise, that wee were not able to heare one another speake. Furthermore, wee were not able to set our feet on the ground, but either on Fowles or Egges which lay so thicke in the grasse: Wee laded two Boats full in the space of three houres, to our great refreshing."

—George Percy, *Observations*

"And at the little Ile called Monica, we tooke from the bushes with our hands, near 2 hogsheads full of birds in 3 or 4 houres."

—Thomas Studley (and others), *The Proceedings of the English Colonie in Virginia . . .*

[13]

LEAVING THE WEST INDIES

April 10, 1607.

After nineteen days in the West Indies the colonists departed and sailed northward:

"The tenth day we set saile and disimboged out of [departed from] the West Indies, and bare our course Northerly."

—George Percy, *Observations*

CROSSING THE TROPIC OF CANCER

April 14, 1607.

"The fourteenth day we passed the Tropicke of Cancer."

—George Percy, *Observations*

A VIOLENT STORM

April 21, 1607.

On this day disaster to the small fleet by a spring squall was narrowly averted:

"The one and twentieth day, about five a clocke at night there began a vehement tempest, which lasted all the night, with winds, raine, and thunders in a terrible manner. Wee were forced to lie at Hull that night, because we thought wee had beene neerer land then wee were."

—George Percy, *Observations*

Cape Henry, Virginia
Site of the First Landing of the Jamestown Colonists on the American Mainland, April 26, 1607

THE FIRST LANDING IN VIRGINIA NEAR CAPE HENRY;

On a beautiful Sabbath day in late April the coast of Virginia was sighted about four o'clock in the morning—19 weeks after the three ships left London and 16 days after their departure from the West Indies. About 30 of the men landed and explored a short distance inland. Master Percy related the events which unfolded during ·the daylight hours of this busy and momentous day:

"The six and twentieth day of Aprill, about foure a clocke in the morning, wee descried the Land of Virginia: the same day wee entred the Bay of Chesupioc directly, without any let or hinderance; there wee landed and discovered a little way, but wee could find nothing worth the speaking of, but faire meddowes and goodly tall Trees, with such Fresh-waters running through the woods, as I was almost ravished at the first sight thereof."

[15]

VIRGINIA INDIANS ATTACKING THE COLONISTS AT CAPE HENRY

APRIL, 26, 1607 "At night when we were going aboard, there came the Savages creeping on all foure, from the Hills, like Beares, with their Bowes in their mouths: charged us very desperatly in the faces ...."

ENMITY OF THE VIRGINIA INDIANS; OPENING THE SEALED BOX.

The first encounter with the Virginia Indians seemed to be a foreboding one, as Captain Gabriel Archer, Gentleman, and Mathew Morton, a sailor, were wounded by the aborigines:

"At night, when wee were going aboard, there came the Savages creeping upon all foure, from the Hills like Beares, with their Bowes in their mouthes, charged us very desperately in the faces, hurt Captain Gabriel Archer in both his hands, and a sayler in two places of the body very dangerous. After they had spent their Arrowes, and felt the sharpnesse of our shot, they retired into the Woods with a great noise, and so left us."

—George Percy, *Observations*

Captain John Smith and Thomas Studley gave only brief accounts of the first landing on the sandy shore of Virginia near Cape Henry:

". . . the first land we made, wee fell with Cape Henry, the verie mouth of the Bay of Chissiapiacke, which at that present we little expected, having by a cruell storme bene put to the Northward.

"Anchoring in this Bay twentie or thirtie went ashore with the Captain, and in comming aboard, they were assalted with certaine Indians, which charged them within Pistoll shot: in which conflict, Captaine Archer and Mathew Morton were shot: whereupon Captaine Newport seconding them, made a shot at them, which the Indians little respected, but having spent their arrowes retyred without harme."

—John Smith, *A True Relation . . .*

"The first land they made, they called Cape Henry; *where anchoring, Maister Wingfield, Gosnoll, and* Newport, *with 30 others recreating themselves on shore, were assalted by 5 Salvages; who hurt 2 of the English very dangerously."*

—Thomas Studley (and others), *The Proceedings of the English Colonie in Virginia . . .*

On the night of April 26 the sealed box was opened —which contained the names of the members of the Council and instructions to be followed by the colonists. Although Percy did not mention this historic event, both Smith and Studley related the incident:

"And in that place [near Cape Henry] was the Box opened, wherein the Counsell for Virginia was nominated. . . ."

—John Smith, *A True Relation . . .*

"That night [April 26, 1607], was the box opened, and the orders read: in which Bartholomew Gosnoll, Edward Wingfield, Christopher Newport, John Smith, John Ratcliffe, John Martin, and George Kendall, *were named to bee the Councell, and to choose a President amongst them for a yeare, who with the Councell should governe. Matters of moment were to be examined by a Jurie, but determined by the major part of the Councell in which the Precedent had 2 voices."*

—Thomas Studley (and others), *The Proceedings of the English Colonie in Virginia . . .*

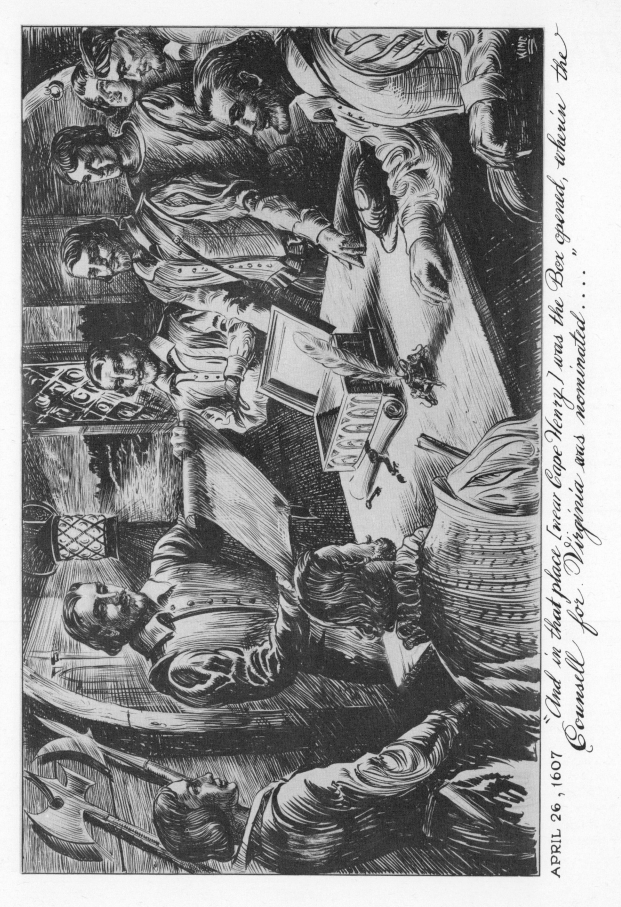

APRIL 26, 1607   "And in that place where I was the Box opened, wherein the Counsell for Virginia was nominated . . . . ."

The Search for A Settlement Site

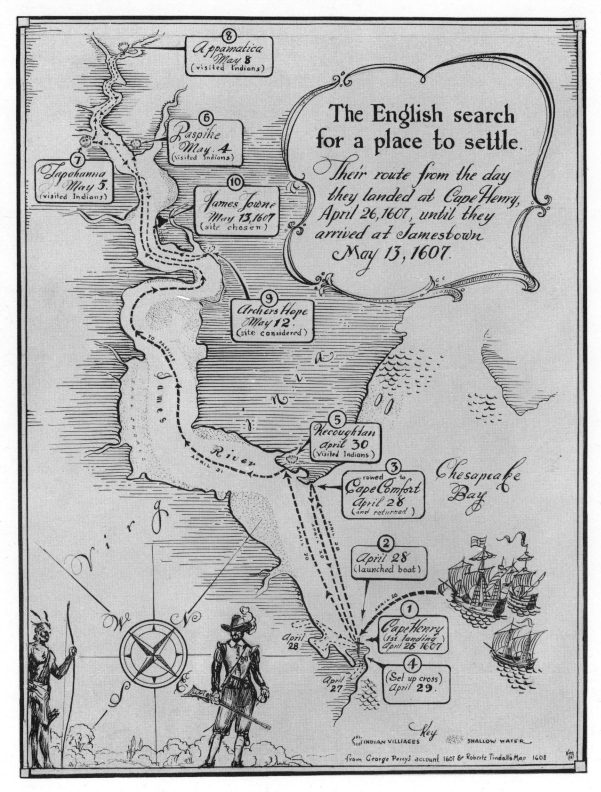

The English search for a place to settle.

Their route from the day they landed at Cape Henry, April 26, 1607, until they arrived at Jamestown May 13, 1607.

8 — Appamatica May 8 (visited Indians)

6 — Paspihe May 4 (visited Indians)

7 — Tapahanna May 5 (visited Indians)

10 — James Towne May 13, 1607 (site chosen)

9 — Archers Hope May 12 (site considered)

5 — Kecoughtan April 30 (visited Indians)

3 — rowed to Cape Comfort April 28 (and returned)

Chesapeake Bay

2 — April 28 (launched boat)

1 — Cape Henry (1st landing) April 26 1607

4 — (Set up cross) April 29

April 28

April 27

TO PASPIHE

James River

Virginia

JAMESTOWN SHORE

APRIL 21

APRIL 30

APRIL 26

Key — INDIAN VILLIAGES — SHALLOW WATER

from George Percy's account 1607 & Roberte Tindall's Map 1608

OYSTERS LEFT BY INDIANS EATEN

Work Begun on Construction of Small Boat; Exploration Inland

April 27, 1607.

During this second day in Virginia, at Cape Henry, the colonists began building a small boat known as a shallop. It appears that the ready-cut timbers were brought from England, as the boat was completed the following day. Perhaps it was the first prefabricated vessel assembled in the New World. On this Monday the settlers also explored inland for about eight miles, and found and ate some roasted oysters left by the Indians.

Only George Percy described the activities of this day, as well as the adventures of the colonists during the next 16 days—when the Englishmen searched for a suitable place in which to plant their colony. Percy's account of what happened on this twenty-seventh day of April:

"The seven and twentieth day we began to build up our Shallop: the Gentlemen and Souldiers marched eight miles up into the Land, we could not see a Savage in all that march, we came to a place where they had made a great fire, and had beene newly a rosting Oysters: when they perceived our comming, they fled away to the Mountaines, and left many of the Oysters in the fire: wee eat some of the Oysters, which were very large and delicate in taste."

—George Percy, *Observations*

Colonists launching their newly-built boat at Cape Henry, April 28, 1607.

A BUSY DAY FILLED WITH EXCITING ADVENTURES

April 28, 1607.

This was a busy spring day full of exciting events. Each adventure was described by the observant chronicler, George Percy, Gentleman. From sunrise to sunset the Englishmen:

(1) Launched their small boat; explored up the bay.

"... we lanched our Shallop, the Captaine and some Gentlemen went in her, and discovered up the Bay, we found a River on the Southside running into the Maine; we entered it and found it very shoald water, not for any Boats to swim ..."

Colonists examining an Indian canoe near Cape Henry.

April 28, 1607.

(2) Found an Indian canoe.

"... Wee went further into the Bay, and saw a plaine plot of ground where we went on Land, and found the place five mile in compasse, without either Bush or Tree, we saw nothing there but a Cannow, which was made out of the whole tree, which was five and fortie foot long by the Rule ..."

The mussels and oysters were thick as stones.

April 28, 1607.

(3) Gathered oysters and clams.
"*Upon this plot of ground we got good store of Mussels and Oysters, which lay on the ground as thicke as stones.*"

Finding pearls in oysters.

April 28, 1607.

(4) Finding pearls.
"Wee opened some [oysters], and found in many of them Pearles."

The savages had been burning the grass.

April 28, 1607.

(5) Marched three or four miles into the woods.

"*Wee marched some three or foure miles further into the Woods, where we saw great smoakes of fire. Wee marched to those smoakes and found that the Savages had beene there burning downe the grasse, as wee thought either to make their plantation [village] there, or else to give signes to bring their forces together, and so to give us battell.*"

[25]

we came into a little plat of ground

The Colonists find a field full of large strawberries.

April 28, 1607.

(6) Marvelled at the wild flowers, trees and strawberries.

"We past through excellent ground full of Flowers of divers kinds and colours, and as goodly trees as I have seene, as Cedar, Cipresse, and other kindes: going a little further we came into a little plat of ground full of fine and beautifull Strawberries, four times bigger and better then ours in England."

[26]

"..we named that point of Land, Cape Comfort"

Approaching Cape Comfort.

April 28, 1607.

(7) Returned to their ships.

"When it grew to be towards night we stood backe to our Ships, we sounded and found it shallow water for a great way, which put us out of all hopes for getting any higher with our Ships, which road at the mouth of the River [the James]."

(8) Rowed over to a point of land which they named Cape Comfort.

"Wee rowed over to a point of Land, where wee found a channell, and sounded six, eight, ten, or twelve fathom; which put us in good comfort. Therefore wee named that point of Land, Cape Comfort."

—George Percy, *Observations*

[27]

From a painting by Stephen Reid in the Norfolk Museum of Arts and Sciences, Norfolk, Virginia

ERECTING A CROSS AT CAPE HENRY

April 29, 1607.

In all probability the men who rowed over to Cape Comfort returned to their small fleet (anchored at Cape Henry) late in the evening, or at night, April 28. The following day—April 29—the settlers gave thanks to their Creator by erecting a cross at Cape Henry:

"The nine and twentieth day we set up a Crosse at Chesupioc Bay, and named that place Cape Henry."
—George Percy, *Observations*

While erecting the cross the colonists may have been mindful of certain instructions given them by the Virginia Company of London:

"Lastly and chiefly the way to prosper and achieve good success is to make yourselves all of one mind for the good of your country and your own, and to serve and fear God the Giver of all Goodness, for every plantation which our Heavenly Father hath not planted shall be rooted out."

VISIT TO THE INDIAN VILLAGE OF KECOUGHTAN

April 30, 1607.

On April 30 the small fleet left Cape Henry and sailed across Chesapeake Bay to Cape Comfort. Anchoring in a small bay (near present day Hampton, Virginia) the shallop was manned, and Captain Newport and some of his men rowed to the Indian village of Kecoughtan. It was the first time the settlers had met the Virginia Indians face to face on friendly terms. How strange and awesome the painted aborigines must have looked to the white men! The Englishmen probably stayed at Kecoughtan for a day or two,

as Percy described the manners and customs of the Indians in some detail, and related many interesting things which happened during this amicable meeting between the whites and the redmen:

(1) First sight of the savages running on the shore:
"Thirtieth day, we came with our ships to Cape Comfort; where wee saw five Savages running on the shoare . . ."

—George Percy, *Observations*

"... *they saw the Captain lay his hand on his heart*."

Meeting the Kecoughtan Indians.

April 30, 1607.

(2) Invitation of the Indians to visit their village:

"... *presently the Captaine caused the shallop to be manned, so rowing to the shoare, the Captaine called to them in signe of friendship, but they were at first very timersome, until they saw the Captain lay his hand on his heart: upon that they laid down their Bowes and Arrowes, and came very boldly to us, making signes to come a shoare to their Towne, which is called by the Savages, Kecoughtan.*"

—George Percy, *Observations*

[30]

"Wee coasted to their Town,..."

The Indians swam with their bows and arrows in their mouths.

April 30, 1607.

(3) The strange manner of the Indians swimming with bows and arrows in their mouths:

"Wee coasted to their Town, rowing over a River running into the Maine, where these Savages swam over with their Bowes and Arrowes in their mouthes."

—George Percy, *Observations*

An Indian Ceremony.

April 30, 1607.

(4) A strange Indian ceremony and feast:
"*When we came over to the other side, there was a many of other Savages which directed us to their Towne, where we were entertained by them very kindly. When we came first a Land they made a dolefull noise laying their faces to the ground, scratching the earth with their nailes. We did thinke that they had*

"... brought us such dainties as they had"

An Indian Feast.

beene at their Idolatry. When they had ended their Ceremonies, they went into their houses and brought out mats and laid upon the ground, the chiefest of them sate all in a rank: the meanest sort brought us such dainties as they had, & of their bread which they make of their Maiz or Gennea wheat, they would not suffer us to eat unlesse we sate down, which we did on a Mat right against them."
—George Percy, Observations

Smoking Indian Tobacco.

April 30, 1607.

(5) Their use of tobacco:

"After we were well satisfied they gave us of their Tabacco, which they tooke in a pipe made artificially of earth as ours are, but far bigger, with the bowle fashioned together with a piece of fine copper."

—George Percy, *Observations*

An Indian Dance.

April 30, 1607.

(6) Their manner of dancing:

"After they had feasted us, they shewed us, in welcome, their manner of dancing, which was in this fashion: one of the Savages standing in the midst singing, beating one hand against another, all the rest dancing about him, shouting, howling, and stamping against the ground, with many Anticke tricks and faces, making noise like so many Wolves or Devils. One thing of them I observed; when they were in their dance they kept stroke with their feet just one with another, but with their hands, heads, faces, and bodies, every one of them had a severall gesture: so they continued for the space of halfe an houre. When they had ended their dance, the Captaine gave them Beades and other trifling Jewells."
—George Percy, *Observations*

"They hang through their ears, fowls legs;"

A Kecoughtan Indian.

April 30, 1607.

(7) Their dress and use of paint:

"They hang through their eares Fowles legs: they shave the right side of their heads with a shell, the left side they weare of an ell long [about 45 inches] tied up with an artificiall knot, with a many of Foules feathers sticking in it. They goe altogether naked, but their privities are covered with Beasts skinnes beset commonly with little bones, or beasts teeth: some paint their bodies blacke, some red, with artificiall knots of sundry lively colours, very beautifull and pleasing to the eye, in a braver fashion then they in the West Indies."

—George Percy, *Observations*

[36]

EXPLORATORY TRIP UP THE JAMES RIVER—FROM KECOUGHTAN TO PASPIHE

April 31 to May 4, 1607.

It is not clear which day the colonists left the Indian village of Kecoughtan, but it is believed to have been either April 31 or May 1. The distance between Kecoughtan and Paspihe village (the next place mentioned by Percy) by way of the winding James River is approximately 50 miles. En route to Paspihe the colonists sailed by the low-lying island which was to be their future home, but whether or not they stopped to visit the beautiful area of woods and swamps is not known. Three miles long by one mile wide, and jutting out prominently from the north side of the wide tidal river, the island must have been observed by Captain Newport and the men in his charge.

Whether or not all three ships in the small fleet sailed as far upriver as Paspihe Indian village is not known. One of the vessels may have remained in one of the sheltered bays between Kecoughtan and Jamestown Island, or all may have sailed together up the wide river (known as Powhatan by the aborigines), named the James by the English after their King and sovereign.

Percy mentioned the visit to Paspihe, an Indian village which was located about 8 miles upriver from Jamestown Island:

"*The fourth day of May, we came to the King or Werowance of Paspihe: where they entertained us with much welcome; an old Savage made a long Oration, making a foule noise, uttering his speech with a vehement action, but we knew little what they meant. Whilst we were in company with the Paspihes, the Werowance [chief] of Rapahanna came from the other side of the River in his Cannoa: he seemed to take displeasure of our being with the Paspihes: he would faine have had us come to his Towne, the Captaine was unwilling; seeing that the day was so far spent he returned backe to his ships for that night.*"

Little did the colonists realize on that fourth day of May that the Paspihes, who claimed the land in the vicinity of Jamestown, would become their mortal enemies and, on more than one occasion, would attempt to wipe out the small English settlement.

"*He seemed to take displeasure.*"

Visiting the Paspihe Indians.

[37]

INVITATION TO VISIT THE INDIAN VILLAGE OF TAPAHANOCK

CALLED RAPAHANNA BY PERCY; QUIYOUGHCOHANOCKS BY CAPTAIN JOHN SMITH

May 5, 1607.

On this day the settlers—still searching for a suitable site for planting a colony—crossed the James River from Paspihe village (not far from where the Chickahominy river runs into the James) to the south shore and visited the Tapahanock Indians, erroneously called the Rapahannas by George Percy. The English spent at least one day at the village (May 5), and perhaps part of the following day. A few of many incidents which took place were reported by the very observant Percy:

(1) Invitation from the chief of the Tapahanocks to visit his village:
"The next day, being the fift of May, the Werowance [chief] of Rapahanna sent a Messenger to have us come to him. We entertained the said Messenger, and gave him trifles which pleased him . . ."

—George Percy, *Observations*

Captain Newport arms his men.

May 5, 1607.

(2) The caution of Captain Newport in sending armed men to the village:
"Wee manned our shallop with Muskets and Targatiers [men armed with shields or light armour] sufficiently: this said Messenger guided us where our determination was to goe."

—George Percy, *Observations*

The Werowance of Rapahanna came down to the water

The Rapahanna (Tapahanock) Indians greet the English—May 5, 1607.

May 5, 1607.

(3) A description of the chieftain and his "goodly men":

"When wee landed, the Werowance of Rapahanna came downe to the water side with all of his traine, as goodly men as any I have seene of Savages or Christians: the Werowance comming before them playing on a Flute made of a Reed, with a Crown of Deares haire colloured red, in fashion of a Rose fastened about his knot of haire, and a great Plate of Copper on the other side of his head, with two long Feathers in fashion of a paire of Hornes placed in the midst of his Crowne. His body was painted all with Crimson, with a Chaine of Beads about his necke, his faced painted blew, besprinkled with silver Ore as wee thought, his eares all behung with Braslets of Pearle, and in either

[40]

eare a Birds Claw through it beset with fine Copper or Gold, he entertained us in so modest a proud fashion, as though he had beene a Prince of civill government, holding his countenance without laughter or any such ill behaviour; he caused his Mat to be spred on the ground, where he sate downe with a great Majestie, taking a pipe of Tabacco: the rest of his company standing about him. After he had rested a while he rose, and made signes to us to come to his Towne: Hee went formost, and all the rest of his people and our selves followed him up a steepe Hill where his Palace was settled."

—George Percy, *Observations*

[41]

"Wee went through the goodliest cornefields."

May 5, 1607.

(4) The Indian corn fields:

"*Wee passed through the Woods in fine paths, having most pleasant Springs which issued from the Mountaines: Wee also went through the goodliest Corne fieldes that ever was seene in any Countrey.*"

—George Percy, *Observations*

The Rapahanna (Tapahanock) Village.

May 5, 1607.

(5) Entertainment by the chief:

"When wee came to Rapahannos Towne, he entertained us in good humanitie."
—George Percy, *Observations*

...There came many stout and able Savages...

VISIT TO THE INDIAN VILLAGE OF APAMATICA

May 8, 1607.

On May 8 the colonists continued their exploring trip westward up the James River, sailing from Rapahanna (Tapahanock) village to the Indian village of Apamatica. The latter place was located on the south shore of the James, on a neck of land formed by the first bend in the river above the mouth of the Appomattox, about 38 miles above Jamestown by water. None of the English observers related how long the settlers stayed at Apamatica, but as the Indians were not overly friendly the visit probably did not exceed a day or two. Only Master Percy described the visit to Apamatica:

"The eight day of May we discovered up the River. We landed in the Countrey of Apamatica, at our landing, there came many stout and able Savages to resist us with their Bowes and Arrowes, in a most warlike manner, with the swords at their backes beset with sharpe stones, and pieces of yron able to cleave a man in sunder. Amongst the rest one of the chiefest standing before them crosselegged, with his Arrow readie in his Bow in one hand, and taking a Pipe of Tobacco in the other, with a bold uttering of his speech, demanded of us our being there, willing us to bee gone. Wee made signes of peace, which they perceived in the end, and let us land in quietnesse."

—George Percy, *Observations*

Apamatica was the last Indian village visited by the English before they planted their colony at Jamestown. It was the most westerly point reached by the colonists up the James River during their search for a settlement site.

VISIT TO ARCHERS HOPE, A POINT OF LAND NEAR JAMESTOWN ISLAND

May 12, 1607.

Between May 8 and May 12 the colonists sailed down the James River and undoubtedly visited many of the attractive bays, inlets, and peninsulas in search for a suitable settlement site. On May 12 they reached a point of land located about 45 miles downriver from the Indian village of Apamatica and three miles below Jamestown Island. (It was the second time the English passed by the Island which was to be their future home.) They named the point of land Archers Hope after one of their group, Captain Gabriel Archer. Located on the north side of the James, the advantages of the forested area impressed the settlers. Percy commented on its good soil, excellent timber, and strategic location; and if the ships had been able to ride near the shore the English undoubtedly would have planted their colony there. Percy described the point of land:

"*The twelfth day we went backe to our ships, and discovered a point of Land, called Archers Hope, which was sufficient with a little labour to defend our selves against any Enemy. The soile was good and fruitfull, with excellent good Timber. There are also great store of Vines in bignesse of a mans thigh, running up to the tops of the Trees in great abundance. We also did see many Squirels, Conies, Black Birds with crimson wings, and divers other Fowles and Birds of divers and sundrie collours of crimson, Watchet, Yellow, Greene, Murry, and of divers other hewes naturally without any art using.*

"*We found store of Turkie nests and many Egges, if it had not beene disliked, because the ship could not ride neere the shoare, we had setled there to all the Collonies contentment.*"

—George Percy, *Observations*

The soil was good

Archers Hope, where the Colonists wanted to settle.

The long voyage and search for a settlement site was about to end. For on the evening of May 13 the three small ships would drop anchor six miles upriver from Archers Hope, near the western end of Jamestown Island.

The *Susan Constant*, *Godspeed*, and *Discovery* reach Jamestown Island, May 13, 1607.

Copy of a painting by Griffith Bailey Coale, in the Virginia State Capitol Building, Richmond.

The Colonists moor their ships to trees: the end of the Voyage.

ARRIVAL AT JAMESTOWN ISLAND—MAY 13, 1607

May 13, 1607.

Although never realized by the pioneer settlers, this May 13 was a momentous day in our nation's history. Late in the evening, when the shadows were lengthening, the small band of adventurous Englishmen reached the low-lying island where, on the morrow, they would plant their colony. As darkness was approaching the colonists decided to spend the night aboard the seaworthy vessels. The three ships, riding in six fathoms of water, were moored to trees—as reported by Master Percy:

"The thirteenth day, we came to our seating place in Paspihas Countrey, some eight miles from the point of Land which I made mention before: where our shippes doe lie so neere the shoare that they are moored to the Trees in six fathom water."

—George Percy, *Observations*

Although there were no Indian villages on Jamestown Island, the Paspaheghs (a tribe of the Powhatan confederacy living in the vicinity of Jamestown) hunted and fished on the wilderness island. Hiding in the reeds and tall grass, the wily savages undoubtedly observed almost every move made by the colonists during the early days of the settlement.

[47]

The First Day at Jamestown, May 14, 1607. Here was planted the English Colony of which Raleigh and Gilbert dreamed.

THE LANDING; THE PLANTING OF THE FIRST SUCCESSFUL ENGLISH COLONY IN AMERICA

May 14, 1607.

On a beautiful spring day, almost five months after the fleet left London, the colonists landed on the small, uninhabited, wilderness island, which they named Jamestown after their sovereign, James I. Of their hopes and dreams we know so little, except that each man desired to better his condition, acquire a small tract of land and, if possible, find New World commodities which would bring profits. Little did they realize on that pleasant May day that of their group of 105 who would remain at Jamestown, only 38 would be alive eight months later—when the first supply ship would arrive from England.

On this important day, when their tiny settlement was planted, their thoughts must have been hopeful ones. The fragrance of the spring flowers permeated the air; the new yellowish-green leaves of the deciduous trees and shrubs sparkled in the morning sun, vibrant with life and color for another growing season; while the tall evergreen trees which bordered the island swamps formed beautiful backdrops in the New World wilderness.

Percy described the first day in the James River settlement:

"The fourteenth day, we landed all our men; which were set to worke about the fortification, and others some to watch and ward as it was convenient.

"The first night of our landing, about midnight, there came some Savages sayling close to our quarter. Presently there was an alarum given; upon that, the Savages ran away, and we [were] not troubled any more by them that night."

Captain John Smith also related the important day's events:

". . . and arriving at the place [Jamestown] where wee are now seated, the Counsell was sworn, and the President elected, which for that yeare was Maister Edm. Maria Wingfield, where was made choice for our scituation, a verie fit place for the erecting of a great cittie, about which some contention passed betwixt Captaine Wingfield and Captaine Gosnold: notwithstanding, all our provision was brought a shore, and with as muche speede as might bee wee went about our fortification."

Thomas Studley and his collaborators emphasized that all members of the colony worked hard when the settlement was first established. They also mentioned the nature of their work:

"Untill the 13 of May, they sought a place to plant in: then the Councell was sworne, Maister Wingfield was chosen President, and an oration made, whie Captaine Smith was not admitted of the Councell as the rest.

"Now falleth every man to worke, the Councell contrive the Fort, the rest cut downe trees to make place to pitch their Tents; some provide clapbord to relade the ships; some make gardens, some nets, &c. . . ."

Thus the English colony was planted and the adventures in the Virginia forest begun. What would be the fate of the new settlement—another Fort Raleigh, lost and engulfed by the mysterious wilderness? Only time would tell.

Today we know the answer. For on the western tip of the small James River island, over 350 years ago, was planted the first successful English settlement in the New World. On the banks of a beautiful Virginia tidal river our nation was born, and to the adventurers who established the colony, a debt of gratitude will forever be owed by all freemen.

"...there came Savages"...

The First Night on Jamestown Island—"About midnight there came some savages sayling close to our quarters."

BIBLIOGRAPHY

All three accounts quoted were written by members
of the early Jamestown settlement. They are:

1. "Observations gathered out of a Discourse of the Plantation of the Southerne Colonie in Virginia by the English, 1606. Written by that Honorable Gentleman Master George Percy." First published in *Purchas his Pilgrimes* by Samuel Purchas (London, 1625) vol. 4, pp. 1685-1690. Printed by W. Stansby for H. Fetherstone.

Lyon Gardiner Tyler in his book, *Narratives of Early Virginia, 1606-1625,* gives the following information about George Percy's account:

"The original manuscript is not preserved, and what has come down to us is only an abridgement published for the first time in 1625 by Samuel Purchas, who assigns as a reason for the omissions he made in it that 'the rest is more fully set downe in Cap. Smiths Relations.' . . .It presents the fullest account we have of the voyage and of the first events of the settlement, to Newport's departure, June 22, 1607. . . ."

Title page reproduced through the courtesy of the William L. Clements Library, University of Michigan, Ann Arbor, Michigan.

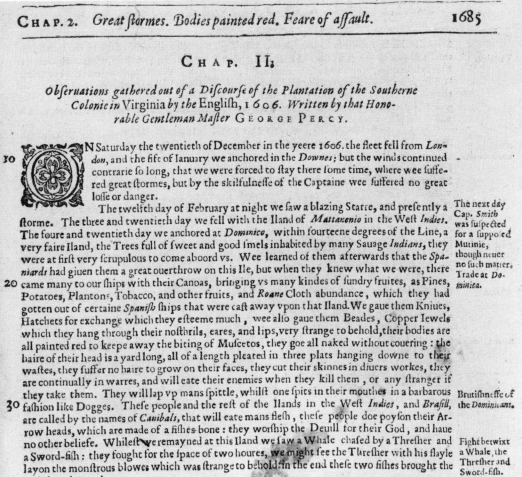

[51]

2. *A True Relation of such occurrences and accidents of noate as hath hapned in Virginia since the first planting of that Collony, which is now resident in the South part thereof, till the last returne from thence. Written by Captaine Smith Coronell of the said Collony, to a worshipfull friend of his in England.* London. Printed for John Tappe, and are to bee solde at the Greyhound in Paules-Church-yard, by W. W. 1608.

This publication is Captain John Smith's first account of the Jamestown settlement.

Title page reproduced through the courtesy of the William L. Clements Library, University of Michigan, Ann Arbor, Michigan.

A TRVE RE-
lation of ſuch occur-
rences and accidents of noate as
hath hapned in Virginia ſince the firſt
planting of that Collony, which is now
reſident in the South part thereof, till
the laſt returne from
thence.

Written by Captaine Smith *Coronell of the ſaid Collony, to a*
worſhipfull friend of his in England.

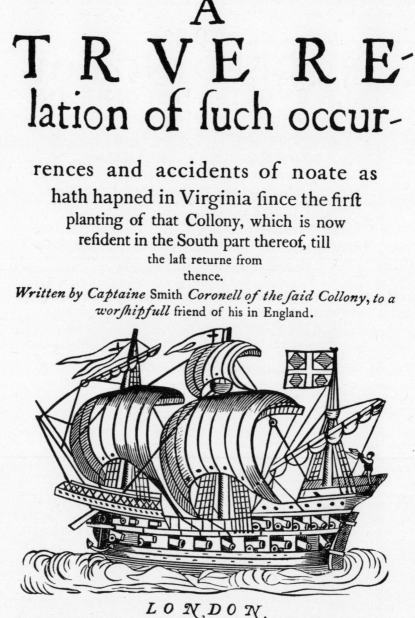

LONDON
Printed for *Iohn Tappe*, and are to bee ſolde at the Greyhound in Paules-Church-yard, by *W. W.*
1 6 0 8

3. *The Proceedings of the English Colonie in Virginia since their first beginning from England in the yeare of our Lord 1606, till this present 1612, with all their accidents that befell them in their Iournies and Discoveries. Also the Salvages discourses, orations and relations of the Bordering neighbours, and how they became subject to the English. Unfolding even the fundamentall causes from whence have sprang so many miseries to the undertakers, and scandals to the businesse: taken faithfully as they were written out of the writings of Thomas Studley the first provant maister, Anas* Todkill, Walter Russell Doctor of Phisicke, Nathaniell Powell, William Phettyplace, Richard Wiffin, Thomas Abbay, Tho: Hope, Rich: Potts *and the labours of divers other diligent observers, that were residents in Virginia. And perused and confirmed by diverse now resident in England that were actors in this busines. By W. S. At Oxford, Printed by Joseph Barnes. 1612.*

THE
PROCEEDINGS OF
THE ENGLISH COLONIE IN

Virginia ſince their firſt beginning from
England in the yeare of our Lord 1606,
till this preſent 1612, with all their
accidents that befell them in their
Iournies and Diſcoveries.

Alſo the Salvages diſcourſes, orations and relations
of the Bordering neighbours, and how they became ſubiect to the Engliſh.

Vnfolding even the fundamentall cauſes from whence haue ſprang ſo many miſe-
ries to the vndertakers, and ſcandals to the buſineſſe: taken faithfully as they were written out of the writings of Thomas
Studley the firſt provant maiſter, Anas Todkill, Walter
Ruſſell Doctor of Phiſicke, Nathaniell Powell,
William Phettyplace, Richard Wiffin, Thomas Abbay, Tho: Hope, Rich: Potts and
the labours of divers other diligent obſerveis, that were
reſidents in Virginia.

And peruſed and confirmed by diverſe now reſident in
England that were actors in this buſines.
By W. S.

AT OXFORD,
Printed by Joſeph Barnes. 1612.